SHOHEI OHTANI

A Little Golden Book® Biography

By Nicole de las Heras • Illustrated by Toshiki Nakamura

For Griffin, my favorite guy to watch sports with
—N.D.L.H.

A GOLDEN BOOK • NEW YORK

Golden Books
An imprint of Random House Children's Books • A division of Penguin Random House LLC
1745 Broadway, New York, NY 10019 • penguinrandomhouse.com • rhcbooks.com

Library of Congress Control Number: 2024952392
ISBN 979-8-217-11775-8 (trade) — ISBN 979-8-217-11776-5 (ebook)
Manufactured in the United States of America
10 9 8 7 6 5 4 3 2 1

Shohei Ohtani was born on July 5, 1994, in a town now called Oshu in northern Japan. The youngest of three children, Shohei was active and athletic—just like his parents. His father worked at a car manufacturing plant and was an amateur baseball player. His mother was an amateur badminton player.

When Shohei was little, his mother would bring him along to her badminton practice. He had a natural talent for swinging a racket.

He started playing baseball in the second grade and was just as good at swinging a bat. Soon, Shohei became a "yakyu shonen" which is Japanese for "baseball boy," or a kid who eats, sleeps, and breathes baseball—it was all he wanted to do!

Shohei showed signs of becoming a real slugger in Little League. To the amazement of his teammates, he would often hit balls that flew past the outfield and into the river!

Shohei's dad was one of his coaches throughout elementary and junior high school. He taught his son many things, including how to hit the ball with the thickest part of the bat and how to bat both left-handed and right-handed. Most importantly, he taught Shohei to be a good sport and teammate on and off the field.

Shohei went to Hanamaki Higashi High School. Even though the school was close to his home, the kids on the baseball team lived on campus for most of the year. The coach made sure his athletes trained hard for success but also kept them humble by giving them jobs such as cleaning the dorm toilets.

Training for the baseball players included swimming, and Shohei was a terrific swimmer. In high school, he was so fast in the pool that his coach believed he could have been on the Olympic swim team. But baseball was what he loved. Shohei was still a yakyu shonen.

He was a star player, setting a Japanese high school record for pitching a ninety-nine-mile-an-hour fastball! Shohei throws with his right hand and settled into batting as a lefty. He became a powerful hitter and is a speedy base runner.

Shohei turned pro after high school. He was the number one draft pick for the Hokkaido Nippon-Ham Fighters. The team offered Shohei the chance to be a two-way player—a pitcher on defense and a designated hitter on offense. This kind of athlete is rare in baseball because very different skills are needed for each position.

He played in Japan for five seasons and was one of the most popular players as well as a league leader at pitching and hitting. One time, he even hit a ball straight through the roof of the Tokyo Dome!

OHTA

In December 2017, the twenty-three-year-old signed a contract with the Los Angeles Angels and moved to the United States. It was always Shohei's goal to play in Major League Baseball (MLB). Excited fans were soon comparing him to another MLB two-way player: the legendary Babe Ruth.

Shohei was awarded Rookie of the Year in 2018. His next two seasons didn't go as planned due to several injuries, but he turned things around for the 2021 season, winning his first league MVP trophy! He was nicknamed "Shotime" because of all the excitement he brought to the game.

Shohei stays in shape by working out, eating well, and getting *lots* of sleep. He aims for ten hours every night and has a two-hour nap before a game.

He is also known to travel with a mattress and pillow made especially for him based on his body measurements.

In 2023, after six years with the Angels, Shohei signed a $700 million, ten-year deal to play for the Los Angeles Dodgers. At the time, it was the biggest sports contract ever!

Shohei likes to keep his life outside of baseball private. He surprised his teammates and fans in February 2024 when he announced that he got married. His wife, Mamiko Tanaka, is a former professional basketball player from Japan. She can often be seen in the stands cheering for her husband.

LA
Dodgers

An injury kept Shohei from pitching during his first season with the Dodgers, but his batting and base running set records. On September 19, 2024, Shohei became the first and only player to hit fifty home runs and steal fifty bases in a single season, making him the founding member of the 50-50 Club. Amazing!

LA
Dodgers
Dodgers
Dodgers
Dodgers

That same season, Shohei accomplished another longtime goal: winning the World Series! The championship matchup between the Dodgers and the New York Yankees wasn't just big news in America—millions of people in Japan watched the games on TV to root for their hometown hero! Since the US and Japan are in different time zones, fans there were eating breakfast when they saw Shohei and the Dodgers beat the Yankees.

The baseball stars returned home to Los Angeles where they were celebrated with a champions parade. Shohei's beloved dog, Decoy, joined in the fun.

Decoy is a fan favorite! The pup got to "throw out" the first pitch at a Dodgers game, and there is even a bobblehead of Shohei holding him!

Shohei Ohtani might just be the greatest baseball player of all time. He still loves the game as much as he did when he was a little yakyu shonen. He always does his very best to help his team win and bring joy to his fans around the world.

What records will Shohei break next?